Mia Discovers

VENICE

by Alexandria Pereira

AuthorHouse™
1663 Liberty Drive
Bloomington, IN 47403
www.authorhouse.com
Phone: 833-262-8899

Because of the dynamic nature of the Internet, any web addresses or links contained in this book may have changed since publication and may no longer be valid. The views expressed in this work are solely those of the author and do not necessarily reflect the views of the publisher, and the publisher hereby disclaims any responsibility for them.

Cover art by Jen Milton

This book is printed on acid-free paper.

ISBN: 978-1-6655-3885-5 (sc)
ISBN: 978-1-6655-3884-8 (hc)
ISBN: 978-1-6655-3886-2 (e)

Library of Congress Control Number: 2021919355

Print information available on the last page.

Published by AuthorHouse 09/22/2021

authorHOUSE®

The Mystery of History Series

Book 2 of 4

Dedication

**To my grandma, for her constant
encouragement, wisdom, and love**

"Hey Grandma, where do I come from?" asked Mia.

"I am so glad you asked," replied Grandma. "You know that you are part of a family. Your mother is my child, and my mother is your great-grandmother. She had a mother too. You have so many, many, grandmothers that we cannot even count them all," said Grandma.

"Where did they all come from?" asked Mia.

"Oh, so you want to know our history," said Grandma.

"Yes, it's a mystery to me," said Mia.

"You see, history is the story of what happened before today—what happened a week ago, a month ago, and so, so many years ago. History is a lot of fun because it tells the story of how people lived and learned new things. Every person who lived before us added to who we are, what we know, and what we can do. Did you know that there was a time when there was no television nor Internet? People didn't even have phones. Would you like to know more?" said Grandma.

"Yes, please," said Mia.

"Then Mia, let's visit the museum today and learn about our history.

"A very, very long time ago, things were different than they are today. Look, Mia, this statue represents one of our first grandmothers. She lived 3 million years ago, and was the first of us to walk on two legs. We call her *Lucy*," said Grandma.

"Grandma, did I come from Lucy?" asked Mia.

"Yes, Mia. She is our ancestor.

AUSTRALOPITHECUS AFARENSIS

Homo sapiens neanderthalensis

"Grandma Lucy had children, and they had children, and then they had children, and then many, many generations later, those children looked like this. These people are called Neanderthals.

"For thousands and thousands of years, these people lived on the land. They caught fish in the rivers and lakes and ate from the many plants that grew all over the country we now call Italy. There were no houses or stores. Each of our grandmothers learned new ways to help her family find food and stay dry and warm. She ground grain with stones, and then later used a metal called bronze to hunt and cut up food.

"As more and more people were born, they worked together to plant crops, and build houses and towns. Then one man, Attila the Hun, wanted people's houses, and food for himself. He and his army fought the people and took their houses and food from them. As Attila and his army were fighting, some of the people and some of Attila's soldiers ran away.

"They ran until they found some land at the edge of a lagoon. We now call this lagoon the City of Venice. There they stayed, worked together, built small houses, planted crops, and fished.

"200 years later another army, called the Lombards, came and tried to take things from the people on the edge of the lagoon. This time the people rowed out into the lagoon on small boats. They stood on a small patch of sand way out in the lagoon where the Lombard soldiers couldn't get to them. The lagoon saved them, and the people cheered," said Grandma.

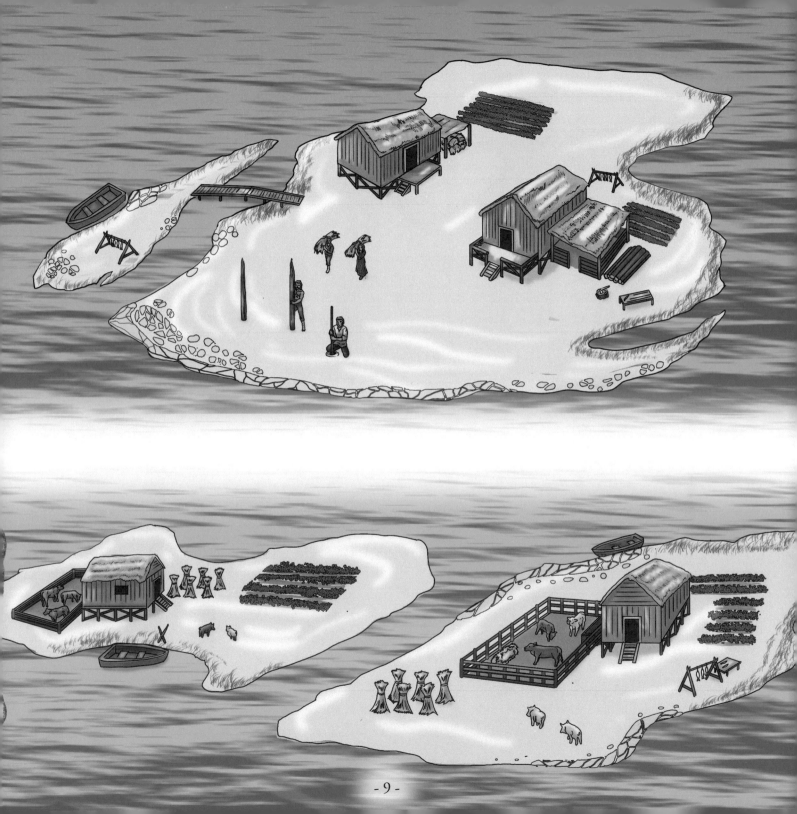

"The people felt safer in the lagoon than on the dry land. So they built their new houses and small farms out on islands they made in the lagoon. The islands were small at first, then grew bigger and bigger. Their houses grew bigger and stronger as well. Some people joined their islands together, and built bridges from one island to the next. That way the next time some armies came to try and take what they had; the people of Venice would be safer.

"As the years went by, the people of Venice continued to work together. The people on Borano Island made lace.

The people on Murano Island made glass.

The people on Arsenol Island made ships and things that go on ships, such as ropes, paddles, oars, and sails. They sailed to other cities and traded the objects they made with people in those cities for things they wanted, such as fancy fabrics, spices, and peacock feathers.

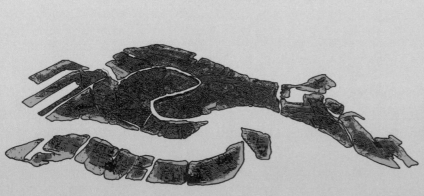

"Mia, I'm getting thirsty," said Grandma.

"Let's get something to drink, Grandma," said Mia.

"Oh, that tastes good. As we are enjoying our drinks, how about I tell you some different things about Venice?" said Grandma.

"OK," said Mia.

"Venice is special and unique just as you are, Mia. Because Venice is a city on the water, they do things differently than we do in cities on land. Venice has no streets, so they ride in small boats, just as we ride in cars. People in Venice ride big boats, just as we ride buses. And their trucks are big boats too. And sometimes, just for fun, they sail on the waters of the lagoon in a gondola.

"Another different thing about Venice is that the dirty water that comes out of the houses and buildings through the pipes pours right into the lagoon. Then a tide of seawater comes in and takes the dirty water out into the ocean. The lagoon is left with fresh seawater. The tide gives the lagoon a big bath two times each day!

"The tide also does something else to Venice once in a while. Sometimes the tide brings in too much seawater for the lagoon to hold. This is called an *acqua alta*. The extra water spills out and over the city and floods it. People have to walk around with high rain boots or on raised wooden platforms to get around the city. The flood does not last long, but it makes getting around in the city very wet and tricky.

"Oh, that was a nice break, Mia. Thank you. Let's keep going," said Grandma.

"Yes, please, Grandma," said Mia.

"Over the centuries the people of Venice continued to sail to other cities, and around the world, trading what they made, for the things they wanted. This made Venice very rich and powerful. But when Venice became greedy and charged too much for the things they made, other cities didn't want Venice to trade with them anymore.

"So, Venice decided to ask the people from the other cities to visit Venice and buy the things they needed. To make it easier for the people to come to Venice, the Venetians built a very long bridge from the end of the land out to one of the islands. On this bridge they built a train track so that a train could bring people to the islands.

"Eventually the Venetians built a road next to the train. Now both trains and cars could bring people to Venice. They still use boats within the city to get around as there still are no streets. Now, people visit from all over the world. They come by car, train, boat, or airplane. They come to buy the things the people of Venice make," said Grandma.

"Wow! Grandma, Venice is super cool! A lot has happened since Grandma Lucy walked on her two legs. I can see all the changes my family made over the centuries so that I could be here today. I'm glad I live in a place with such fun things to learn. My history is no longer a mystery. I live in Italy, and this was my Venetian History. Thank you, Grandma," said Mia.

"You are welcome, Mia," said Grandma

Venetian Timeline

452 AD   Attila the Hun and his army work their way south, leaving behind destruction.

569   Lombard armies invade northern Italy.

726   Venice elects its first doge, a very powerful leader who sets the rules by which Venice would govern itself.

814   Construction begins on many of the houses and buildings we still see along the canals of Venice. The first Doge's Palace is built.

828   Venetian traders in Alexandria, Egypt, steal the bones of Saint Mark and bring them back to Venice.

1094   The Basilica of San Marco is completed, and Saint Mark's bones are buried there.

1094   The first gondolas are used in Venice, a boat specifically designed for the waters of the Venetian Lagoon.

1171   Venice opens its first bank as a site of trading activities.

1204   Venice supplied ships for Crusaders heading to the Holy Land.

1271   Crusaders loot Constantinople, in present-day Turkey, and bring back many treasures. Among them is *Triumphal Quadriga*, the four bronze horses that adorn the front of the Basilica San Marco (copies outside, originals inside).

1340   The Doge's Palace (*Palazzo Ducale*) is rebuilt after a fire burned it down.

1475   The Renaissance finds its way to Venice.

1846   The Venice Railroad Bridge is constructed, linking the mainland to the islands in the lagoon by train and ending the island's primary defense from the land.

1933   The Ponte della Libertà (Liberty Bridge), is completed, allowing cars to travel directly from the mainland to the historical city of Venice out in the lagoon.

1966   A terrible tidal flood occurs on the islands in the lagoon. Many buildings are badly damaged, and some still remain in need of major cleaning or rebuilding.

Today, 5.5 million tourists come visit the historical city each year.

Education Support Activities

Basic Human Needs

food
shelter
clothing
the need to socialize
the need to solve problems, invent, and be creative

Practical Life and Sensorial Foundation

Engage children in activities characteristic of Italy:
plant a seed
wash grapes
sweep outside steps or walkway
hang clothes on a clothes line

History

past, present, and future
timelines

Science

innovation
building and engineering

Geography and Map Work

continents
Europe
significant landforms

Botany

focus on grapes and other agricultural products of Italy

Earth Science

volcanoes

Peace Curriculum

peace table process
conflict resolution skills

Printed in the United States
by Baker & Taylor Publisher Services